TOOLS FOR QUALITY FOR SCHOOLS

DR DHEERAJ MEHROTRA

Contents

PREFACE

Tools For Quality For Schools *is a priority for schools to encapsulate quality culture in action. It has a mechanism of exploring the ideas and strategies to bring out in public the challenges and converting them into solutions on the move.*

The book defines the structural format in action with the inception of quality tools and benchmarked strategies in particular.

Happy learning guys!

Dr Dheeraj Mehrotra

I
Quality In Education

To Teach is to preach. The subjective modulation task the learning regime to years and years of research with leverage of connecting within the learners. Teach children to teach themselves, and foster a love for learning. So, why are there so many students who cave in and quit? Why are the student dropout rates at an astonishingly high rate? Whatever happened to parental involvement and budgets that generally supported a solid, quality education?

To the pride of learning, I ask, what are students expected to learn from their classroom experiences? What do they genuinely need to know to be successful and prepared for college or career readiness? Current research shows that Deep Learning and Close Reading techniques significantly improve academic results for all students involved. How do we, as educators, foster these and other researched-based programs into more schools?

Quality instruction is a vital component of quality education; however, not all learning is acquired and grasped inside the classroom environment. Indeed, teachers should encourage students to explore, be critical thinkers, and become learner-centred. An exceptional teacher focuses upon classroom teaching, community building, and individualized mentorship.

The time says it all, with the inception of technology in education, the page is there for sure. However, irrespective of the perseverance, determination, and patient use of highly qualified educators, ultimately, students will get out of their education what they put in. The philosophical dilemma doesn't exist with the concept of inspiring the already gifted student or illuminating the students who have a passion for learning. The true challenge of teaching is engaging and nurturing the love of learning for all students, especially those who have academically and emotionally "checked out."

The solace remains towards bringing learning within the four walls of the classrooms from the BLACK SCREENS of the kids, desktops, laptops, and now the palmtops via mobile. Students need to attain more than rigorous content objectives. There needs to be a paradigm shift towards less palpable skills and a greater emphasis on creative thinking, collaboration, and problem-solving coupled with thorough teaching and instruction. Students will primarily benefit when they can reflect upon and evaluate ways to improve their overall comprehension. Teachers should also seek beneath and beyond the expectations of standards to teach the whole child.

As a lifelong learner, I take delight in being the student and the teacher. I embrace the challenges of pedagogy and an academic arena of active learning and teamwork. Within quality instruction and education, the framework needs real-world experiences, discussions, analysis, and evaluations.

Far to believe but for sure, Engaging students to be equipped to grasp the material, embrace technology and facilitate classroom dialogue strategically is the pinnacle. The crux of my educational and professional endeavors has fashioned my teaching perspective, and ultimately, students should be at the core of all teaching philosophies. Creativity within classrooms is activated with the perception of engagement with all the kids and not just with the few bright minds. The initiative has to be to catch them young and innocent. It is high time that we approach the mechanism to Teach One- Teach All as a prime scope towards gaining connection with the kids in the classrooms. It is high time we the teachers/ educators start reflecting on our pedagogies with reference to the new age demands and policies.

The children engage and tend to RUN away from Teachers they don't like. They only like the subject if they want the teachers. Hence, it is requisite for all the teachers to bring in a **WOW** *capsule expose' within and outside the classrooms incorporated through creativity and spectrum of learning to learn as a hobby rather than an occasional occurrence. Let learning be creative, experiential above all, fertile. To teach in this VUCA world is greater a challenge for the majority* *today with the march of expectation from the stakeholders. There comes the task to reflect how to make the best in use and the delivery to make it functional for the learners to be engaged and communicative.*

II

Priority Learning

The cyber-based revolution of the learning community has had a dwelling effect on its dwellings and the new age digital learners want speed and where – ever content and assessment of their tasks. This abstract defines and declares an empirical reach on new age demands and necessities to make the learning more

clear, obvious and desirable in the distracting world of today where the children have digitalized themselves of their dependence on technology and self-oriented learning. To the surprise of many, a few years from now, the very iconic symbols of academic delivery, the hardbound books, chalk, duster and above all the desks and tables, may soon become merely a historical representation of the way the teaching was delivered at schools. The tech culture has revolutionised the very means of living and learning and is expected to pound overleaps in time to come bringing more liberty, individuality and choice of learning to the masses. **Technology is now an essential part of our daily world and educators are creatively using it in the classroom and**

beyond. Thanks to the power and governance of Cloud Computing that we tend to deliver a one-stop solution for schools to install and make a role towards Quality integrated with Excellence within the school and its wider spectrum of boundaries in a big way.

Managing the Googlers

There is an urgent need for defines and drafts as essentiality for schools to ponder over the requirement of a cloud presence of their delivery via involvement of all stakeholders. The objective has to make all the stakeholders viz. the students, teachers, parents and the society as a whole, empowered, connected, engaged and successful. What is desired as of now is the combination of a Knowledge Hub Resource proposed by schools with an essence of Knowledge Transfer, Knowledge Sharing and Knowledge Community. The desire and demand for this Knowledge Hub are shared towards feedback and is a proposal to uplift the proposition towards Quality Learning Platform using the three subways viz.

How do we understand where education systems and schools are?

Relating to an aspect of this study, it is fertile to note that the data analysis relates to the continuous LIKES on their social networking platform but in reality and of demand. The scenario has to be fed in real life schooling environments and need to be made public among the intenders of knowledge delivery and sharing under the pretext of making the Learning Happen in classrooms and beyond. The objective has to be to *Cure Ignorance* via collaborations of teacher-led incentives and uploads, there appears a sound preface that we conclude what is a desire and what is a demand by the schools today.

General feedback by teachers and practitioners in the field of education needs to be analysed. Exploring improvement via innovation is a definition of the new framework today. This helps the knowledge vendors to understand the education system and its change being desired at a common pace.

The objective to implement the technology of a complete Knowledge Hub, integrated with sharing, transfer and collaborate, has to have an ultimate provision to deliver the greatest impact on learning, including school management and the best ever classroom delivery and practice the resources which enhance productivity. It is expected to deliver a novel means to the Knowledge

Education Framework via this whole exercise, which delivers, exploration, orientation and deliberations by the teachers who partner to the promotion of their schools. We relate to a common hub to provide a knowledge base to schools on the cloud with easy access to the modules and the information. Here we need to provide definite data security and satisfaction from the end of the clients to promote the learning community with the coordination of Teachers/ Students/ Parents with Management in view of all towards productivity. The hubs designed and propagated regard to a spectrum of Knowledge delivery making each and every student of the school be a collaborator to the knowledge canvas via the cloud. As we rightly believe in the fact that, for education delivery to function and happen, chalk and board are not enough for the teaching system. What is required is a **smile**, an opportunity for the students to **create**, **involve** and **explore** through ICT as the novel ways of understanding the subject further.

Teacher, the Educator should use technology to its fullest of wisdom and capacity available and the cloud format offers him the liberty to work beyond school hours 24x7 with ease of his comfort from home. The sole objective is to explore the magic of a cloud-based learning platform that is changing the way in which teachers and learners are embracing web technologies.

The implementation if explored as a complete knowledge hub would make the teaching/ learning process easy, interesting and result oriented. In the 21st century, a teacher must make efforts for digital learning as technology is not going to replace teachers, but those who don't use technology will be replaced by those who do. Features like uploading and downloading for the stakeholders tend to expertise the learning density in a big way. It is far sound to govern with this capsule but a lot is required to generate from the end of the vendors to provide what is expected and granted initially as a Tailor-Made solution and then ultimately being grounded onto a common fabric towards acceptance in mass.

III

Quality as a Preface

SMS', Groups' via Whatsapp, FB Connect and Skype are some of the means to connect with the community of parents, the ultimate stakeholders of the learning community. The desire to know the updates has come

to concern by many at large. Parents tend to be nurturing teachers of themselves with the pride of being mature decision-makers for the family but their inception towards school leverage counts to nurture the communication expertise to showcase towards excellence. The periodic motion of my child or my ward from the teacher to the parent comes with an ease of perception to a little gap somewhere.

At odd time intervals, the connection is a miss which precludes the success of the children both in terms of knowledge seeker to the skilful attributes of concern. The lamination which reserves because of this has to explore with the empowered and enhanced parent-teacher communication expertise on cards and has a frequent occurrence in particular. Believing in the fact that the parents involvement activates the learning in a big way. To the density of understanding, this involvement caters to the supreme and impacts the outcome of the school education in totality. Bridging this gap is a universally accepted desire for now. The kids who engage themselves among peers to explore learning, tend to deliver and count on the self-learning mode of creative learners and information creation individuals. The database of the knowledge source ware activates their presence of deem interest to the peers. The parents connect hence-forth is a priority as of now and the following ideas and points tend to discover the universality of its acceptance: School Diary/ Almanac to some extent delivers the freedom to share in writing with acknowledgement and share. This is one of the bonds which promote a connection. With the pride and pleasure of many, the Cloud-based Connect has particularly paved to the new dimension *and the definition of connecting with the stakeholders via the word of clue "ERP" which provides a platform that can integrate into the existing pedagogy and frees the teachers/ educators of connect and to make them perform better at their destined assignments.*

Want for connecting, as we the parents, confirm to the engagement in our children's school's education as an observer, the communication and the connect in particular, the limiting belief towards the students by the teachers. The teachers, do have but, the limited time in the classroom with the classroom sizes not paving a fixed number, it appears exclusively impossible to identify the concept of understanding for every student in the classroom itself. No wonder the power of technology has paved a proper instant communication methodology; the limitations preview a different mindset. There appears no way to identify learning levels and customize and distribute content based on those learning levels without changing the way the classroom was taught. The tech candies dwell here with perception and dilute the tension of the masses in most of the unique ways.

With the advancement, the parents are able to connect continuously engage in their child's learning and development through the automated reports, letting them know what was taught in the class, what their child's learning levels are and how they have been progressing in particular. The aimed requisite is to communicate, collate and collaborate in conjunction to deliver the best for the stakeholders, the ultimate google generation of the day, who pact to learn at their leisure and pleasure without the chalk or duster but the pace of their own interest via the communication tool of theirs at prosperity. The ultimate is the spectrum to deliver engagement for the masses within the rooms of knowledge deliver and also in the cyberspace gaining the repute of ORM, the Online Reputation Management for the educators at large. This is a particular fact of soliciting culture to dwell and explore the narration in particular.

The taste of technology has yielded a pace with the march to deviate many schools to come on apps to the surprise of many which offer a certain lookout of connecting with base. I remember the great fable here about the High-Flying Balloons: A man was selling balloons on the streets of New York City. He knew how to attract a crowd before he offered his wares for sale. He took a white balloon, filled it up, and let it float upward. Next, he filled a red balloon and released it. Then he added a yellow one. As the red, yellow and white balloons were floating above his head, the little children gathered around to buy his balloons. A hesitant boy looked up at the balloons and finally asked, "If you filled a black balloon, would it go up too?'. The man looked down and said, 'Why, sure! It's not the colour of the balloon, it's what's inside what makes it go up!'

What's inside of you determines whether you achieve peak success experience in your life. Climbing to the peak depends upon your mind and your attitudes. The learning from the above comes as an essence to learning for motivating our students, to be attracted to positive comments and be ready to excel in life like the high balloons with no colour of choice but the high expectations in particular. Let sky maybe not the limits towards success for it counts to be a Kaizen as a habit rather than an occasional occurrence. For today the teachers' need to connect at length to the parents and the students with equal pace and density of satisfaction to pave their being STREET SMART! with the very connect of doses and learnings of fertilized future of their wards in particular. As for teachers, anger at times is a preface out of irritation within the classroom situations. Let there be a niche of the tale, "Kill Anger before it kills you !", we at times blame different things for losing our temper, let this be off the routine, if there has to be a win-win situation for all, for children will only like the subject if they like the TEACHER!

IV
Quality Circles within Classrooms

The pride of learning counts with the conception of Learning with a special index of education of heart and head in particular. The vital role of education being provided in schools deliver the pace of VALUE education as a parcelled knowledge base towards the masses. It is the education of the soul, believing in the pretext of "Learning to Learn" as a hobby rather than an occasional occurrence.

The holistic education as the word says talks about the overall education of head and heart with wisdom to deliver at pace. It is like knowing self with a belief of human values on priority with four pillars of learning, which includes, learning to learn, learning to know, learning to be and learning to work. The essence is to catch them young and innocent on priority. When we learn with pleasure we never forget. The choice is ours to deliver as teachers and educators to make the delivery and the deliberations in particular through the framework of pleasure and pride at the same time with the spiritual cult and the preface towards values and respect towards all religions of the world.

*Wikipedia rightly defines, holistic education as: "**Holistic education** is a philosophy of **education** based on the premise that each person finds identity, meaning, and purpose in life through connections to the community, to the natural world, and to humanitarian values such as compassion and peace". Hence the unique blend of learning is through the meaningful attribute of knowing the purpose of life and self. The inclusion is about the self and the meaning of life into being alive and getting the* *purpose understood for the self and the objectives narrated towards excellence in particular. Respect for others towards recognition as support needs and connect with the nature, concerns towards the needy and the understanding of the universal brotherhood with implications towards peace and unity should be the concern over acceptance as a universal truth and virtue of life and living in totality.*

Some of the necessities which integrate holistic education relate to the following:

- *Manners*

- *Hands-on Lessons*

- *Core Academics*

- *Emotional Development*

- *Critical Thinking Skills*

- *Conflict Resolution Skills*

- *Character Formation*

Healthy Social Skills

One of the means to garner interest among the students to explore and inherit the essence of holistic attributes is through the inception of Quality circles in particular. Student Quality Circles' (SQC), is a means to develop group learning scenarios within schools. A Quality Circle is a group of people who come together and brainstorm over a common task and develop strategies towards Implementation.

In the field of academics, the concept of SQC has had its inception for over two decades and has taken its shape as one of the enriching tools towards excellence within classrooms.

A Student Quality Circle also known as SQC is a group of 5 to 15 student members, an ideal number is 8, who sit together in the form of a circle and discuss work-related problems. They accordingly evaluate the causes of the selected problem and try solving the same using the various quality tools and finally develop strategies to plan and execute the derivatives.

The encapsulation targets issues related to value system, universal brotherhood and knowing the beliefs and spectrum towards peace and harmony. In addition, the universal values are implemented through means of various interactive sessions in the schools which include the morning assemblies, PTM (Parent Teacher Meetings), Coffee Table with the Head of Schools during Class wise interactions and above all during the Annual Day functions. The initiative should be to imbibe in them the curiosity to learn for life in particular. Some of the advantages which revolve around the holistic attributes within schools relate to the following:

Improve Attention in Class

It is not a secret that many students find it hard to pay attention and concentrate in class. Surprisingly, laziness is not the real reason for this situation. In most cases, it is because stress, worries, fears and personal problems take their focus away from the lessons. This is where mindfulness meditation will play its role. Practising mindfulness can help the students to concentrate better because it directly influences the brain, especially the hippocampus part. And since it jogs the hippocampus to be more active, their memory and critical learning skill will be improved and help them get better grades.

Develop Better Interpersonal Skill

The competition and also pressure to always be the best in class can affect the student's social and emotional skills. They tend to only focus on themselves and don't *care about what's happening around them. Interpersonal skill is very important to survive in the real world. So, the school must make sure that the pressure to perform well in school will not harm their interpersonal skill. Mindfulness training will also make the prefrontal cortex, the part of the brain that regulates emotion, more active. As a result, the students will be able to be more empathetic, more sociable as well as improve their behaviour in school.*

Help Students Coping with Stress

It is very normal for students to experience stress when facing a challenging time in their education. However, the situation of the modern education system often forces the students to experience toxic stress, the kind of stress that can negatively affect their mental health. Stress is normal, but it can be dangerous when the students don't know how to deal with the stress. This is one of the main issues that mindfulness practice can solve. Mindfulness helps the students to see things more objectively and also relax their bodies and mind when facing a stressful situation.

School should not only focus on lessons and grades, but also education for life. The education system should really start to pay attention to the student's mental state too, and mindfulness meditation is one of the best methods for that. It will teach the students to be more mindful of the present, which can help them cope with stress, improve their optimism about life and also their performance in school. Schools do predict and practice innovative ways to deliver passion to the students. The yoga sessions and other mind-based exercises reveal an open spectrum of the level of mindfulness we need in our schools today.

• 22 •

V
Classroom Strategies

The Indian Education System as a result of the widespread illiteracy has its past history now and to the surprise of many, the country has successfully adapted its quality education framework to global standards since Independence. The learning within schools since the Independence has had its say of reputation and choice by the millions of reach. Thanks to the private players who hand in hand projected literacy with the modulated mechanism set via National Education Framework over the years from time to time. We have travelled far from blackboards to digital boards and from Namastay to Hello to Google Framework over the years.

Much of the very best reliable approaches for training analysis have actually headed out of design just recently. A great deal of children fails the fractures due to entire language reviewing programs. Unlike phonics-based analysis, the entire language does not actually provide discovering impaired children the devices to seem out brand-new words. These youngsters, since they do not have an all-natural impulse for checking out that is also created as various other youngsters-- merely never ever discover to review from entire language alone. The schools today unlike yesteryears have a changed adoption of QUALITY as a choice for all the stakeholders particularly the Teachers, Students and Parents at large.

Still, in some cases, exploratory education and learning function much better than a traditional, educator driven version of the class. When pupils are tested to ask concerns and also address troubles, they find out exactly how to assume by themselves. While they're doing this, naturally, they additionally reach establish mathematical, analysis, and also scientific research abilities. It does not help all youngsters, however, it is an excellent program for lots of. Some trainees require an extra organized class, nevertheless, so it is important to separate your time in between various reliable training techniques. This way, both the pupils that such as to pay attention to talks and also those that such as to discover by themselves obtain something. With the increase in the education budget every year, India has been progressing with a wave of QUALITY education of International repute of sense and longevity to its totality.

Being a great instructor indicates finding out reliable training techniques. Numerous instructors like to pick one approach and also persevere at all times. Some individuals design themselves as disciplinarians, counting on an old-fashioned approach of enlightening that calls for outright obedience. Other individuals take a very easygoing strategy, providing their pupils as much flexibility as feasible as well as thinking that knowledge needs to originate from within. The most effective instructors, nonetheless, are the ones that are versatile. They do not have their very own animal efficient mentor approaches. Instead, they agree to take techniques from anywhere that functions.

A great deal of the moments, individuals fail on a reliable training approach. Issues that seem mainly behaviour commonly happen as an outcome of discovering impairments. Youngsters that have problem analysis may begin to act out of stress. The college areas, at the same time, often will certainly capture them acting out without managing the resource of it-- the reality that the youngster cannot check out.

The good news is, there are lots of reliable mentor techniques to assist in finding out handicapped children. Utilizing word checklists, phonics policies, mnemonic tools, as well as several various other academic techniques, these youngsters can find out to check out. Remarkably sufficient, nevertheless, these are likewise several of one of the most efficient training approaches for various other trainees. There are locations where the old approaches are the very best. The priority and recognition to special education, health education, technology in education have all come as a framed mechanism in making our country's educational strata a benchmark for the nations. Long way to go, we the educators have a special and noble spectrum but what is required the most is a special status to the teachers, as nation builders unlike other professions available today. The profession needs special attention and priority over others with many benefits and respect of choices today.

VI

The Wow Educator- Making a difference

Yet simply stating words right into the air whether they are listened to or comprehended truly isn't a mentor is it? Place it in the context of a cook. If you prepare a remarkable dish that is tasty, prepare it with the finest of products as well as existing it with ideal atmosphere, is it still a fascinating dish if there is no one at the table to value it and also no one consumes the dish? No, you are just a cook when the client eats your food and also values every subtlety of the taste and also the experience of appreciating what you have actually done.

Whether that drives you insane relies on whether you think about the act of training total when you talk or when the pupil understands as well as recognizes what you are claiming. Extremely commonly when you see an educator talking you recognize that this instructor has definitely no worry for whether the pupils are obtaining it or otherwise. They do rule out it their work to make certain the pupils recognize or engage with the product. They are a distribution car and also if they proclaim the lecture efficiently, they have efficiently "instructed".

This suggests that you will certainly need to transform your mentor design. It implies that you will not be pleased with simply overcoming a lecture. As a matter of fact, it may lead to the completion of the lecture as a mentoring tool for you totally. To actually learn if those children are paying attention as well as engaging with the product, you will certainly need to alter your strategy to an interactive mentor design.

You will certainly need to begin speaking to pupils or with trainees as well as not AT them. Once you do that, the feedback you will certainly obtain and also the high quality of your training will certainly enhance so drastically, you will certainly never ever intend to return.

That difference is what drives educators insane when they really feel trainees are not paying attention. To an instructor that wants the genuine act of mentor, their work is refrained from doing till the pupils realize the product as well as engage with it, examine it and also lastly understand it as well as make that expertise their very own. A lecture not listened to, not comprehended, not "educated" is not showing in any way, it's simply speaking.

Preparing to end up being an educator has to do with greater than feeling in one's bones exactly how to create a lesson strategy and also exactly how to arrange a course space and also make a bulletin board system. Ending up being an educator implies you turn into one of those fantastic individuals that can take trainees from unenlightened to educated as well as from unenlightened to absolutely "educated". When it is your phoning call to end up being that sort of instructor to simply chat at pupils without any expertise of whether they understand what you are claiming in all is definitely undesirable. There is a sensation that all speakers experience when they are dealing with a group that if you thought of it significantly, it would certainly reach you. It is a sensation that any kind of educator that is attempting to pass on understanding to a space filled with trainees will certainly experience too. As well as if you consider it significantly, it will certainly reach you also. That sensation takes place when you are speaking along and also you watch out at those empty faces gazing up at you and also you recognize that a couple of, some or perhaps every one of those minds behind those faces is paying definitely no focus to you in any way.

VII

The Pride of Learning
in the TECH Age !

Hi, I am a learner to profile my learning to the ultima. I google, I rake for knowledge every now and then to the per se of making the world go the to the heavens

to relate learning as the modulation of the artistic community in regard to making the personality on oneself.

The relates to this encapsulates with far-fetching advances for the exploring which comes via drawing the momentum and spectrum of the new age. For today we don't rate any teacher as a sage on the say, but a facilitator who is just into sharing the knowledge as an interpreter rather than a saint on the stage sharing the unlearning or the unknown for the say. The pride nourishes with talents getting unrolled with the fashion of making the format the solace way and deliver the pride in making the showcase the positive way to benefit the masses in particular.

The Scenario:

The challenging scenario as teachers and learners' rests in making the knowledge delivery the better to perforate with the margin to be different what I was yesterday and what I would be tomorrow in particular. The fragrance checks the desire to make the world go the best way forward with the march to generate the spectrum of Learning to Learn the better strokes with the beneficiary satisfaction in particular. The rays of hope generate with the march of time and tide to laminate the success stories of people becoming

IAS and PCS with the slated limitations as of reviews and predictions. When we come across a part of information we tend relating it to in a behavioral manner, what is missing of say is the very connect with the information, the information provider and the medium which provided the information in regard to the spectrum.

The preface delivers new and positive ways to mediate with the preface of learning via tools and the applications which appear with us as a minute routine, we tend to check our messages, mails, whatsapp features and no one is here to align the same of pride and perfection in particular.

As a learner of the new age we need to be busy and prepared to face the changes and multiply the spectrum towards sharing for the best and making the art and hamper the best to diagnose and relate to adjust.

The classic example lie before us is the grand parents getting to learn about the commuting about distant via skype or any other software and that too from their grand children at ease. Technology has empowered in fact the say to generate the preface in the best possible *manner. The commodities to mention related to decision making with pride and honour, followed with a flavoured inception of knowledge sharing as a personality dwelling feature by the participants.*

The traits of learner relate to new phase of computing to herald the causes and encapsulations in direction of:

a.

What to know?

b.

Where to Know?

c.

What to do after knowing?

d.

Whom to share?

e.

What Next?

The new-age learning comes with the pride and honour of knowing and derivatives with the pace of SIX

MONTHS of age as we march against time in the field of the techno-driven world. Let us all get to learn via the rash of technology and become techno strong rather than just being tech-savvy !

VIII

BE A ROCKSTAR TEACHER!

Rockstar Teachers are not made nor born; they are self-made. The segment which plays the role lies in the word QUALITY. Quality is a word that defines perfection, but alas the word quality for teachers reflect the ready reckoner towards model and a google substitute for the masses of age. The teacher who is a monitoring force behind all the activities within the classroom is reflected re-schedule the learning for we cannot teach the way we were taught.

The sequences reveal that it is more so ever a true explanation to monitor or get monitored for student's sake, with expertise in various fields of knowledge as a requirement rather than an occasional occurrence in totality. The fragrances of desire from a favourite or a rock star teacher pertain to the reality on cards. For the classrooms of today desire, let there be showers of blessings, showers of blessings we pray. The classrooms of today deliver learning not knowledge due to the open learning available to the kids via WWW i.e. Whatever, Whenever and Whatever as an easy means to dose the party spectrum within classrooms.

The shadow of a Teacher, delivers pride and perfection, with the belief of making the world go better and informed. The tools and the e-learning deliver the pace of quality deliberations within classrooms for the children, the generation next, loves the subject only when they like the teachers, their traits and fervour in particular. Students' are not their behaviours and hence labelling them sets them up for failure and can also reflect or affect the self-esteem of the rest of the class. This is a once in a blue moon spectrum, and the reflection of many classroom experiences and routines. The prime objective to deliver a quality environment is paced via paying attention to what your students are doing while you are teaching. The doing may be listening intently, fiddling and doodling, poking others, raising their hand a little, raising their hands, making noises, moving around, quiet but not looking or listening actively and above all sleeping with their eyes open! As teachers, we don't get to decide whether we have challenging students in our classes, but we can certainly decide how we respond to them.

A Quality Teacher is expected to deliver a pace of learning and create a rapport, chat with the students using the languages they understand and also gives them attention at the beginning of the class. He is also expected to encourage them in front of the whole class, noticing the good responses they exhibit and asking them simple questions about the work they are doing. The teachers need to continuously encourage and engage with the colleagues for ideas, with planning and introduction of new topics merging them with the previous learning during class hours.

Quality conception is delivery of more fun at school for the students, mastering the emotions by teachers, learning more effective ways of teaching and above all developing a greater rapport with the students. As rightly quoted by Martin Luther King. Jr. "Intelligence plus character – that is the goal of true education, the teachers to deliver quality and perfection must role out as WOW teachers with pace and time. The personalized learning must equip the teachers' participation of students having active voice on products for assignments. Not only this the students must be motivated to develop learning experiences based on interests and needs, in addition, the students must collaborate with teachers on developing learning tasks and assignments. The readiness and the learning preferences prevail with obvious reasons supporting this fragrance and fertilise the productivity at pace. A teacher is also needed to provide choices based on trend data, must be street smart and by choice, not by chance to make learning fun and entertaining for the masses within classrooms. Of course, to shelter the thought, Teachers make all other professions possible is authentic only when there is a WOW feature within classrooms and children are glued to the eyeballs of the teacher. The new-age spectrum for being a QUALITY Teacher should dwell as LIFE signifying,

L- Love what you do.

I – Be Inspired.

F – Be free to make things better.

E – Make an Effort to learn for the better.

The Literacy is to be re-imagined with HABITUDES, which incorporates the assembly of Habits and

Attitude. The content here applies to derivatives which include Imagination, Curiosity, Self Awareness, Perseverance, Courage, Adaptability and Passion. In addition, use questioning strategies that make all students THINK AND ANSWER. Each day includes some questions you require every student to answer. Find a question you know everyone can answer, and have the class respond all at once. This shall engage the masses and develop their interest in the subject in real!

The above explores a new page of skill development and monitoring of presentation modules engaging the learner in the best of productive manner of the new age requirements of the Continuous and Comprehensive Assessment (CCE) by schools as a mandate. Paying attention to how they learn and their motivation levels is one of the Quality Assessment Tools for Learning to happen. Teachers and Parents need to believe in the saying, 'Some can fly higher than others, But each one flies the best it can. Why compare one against the other? Each one is different. "

Cheers and happy learning.

IX

Increasing Engagement Within Classrooms

Wow, the activated classroom is a fun learning exploring for quality and satisfaction for the kids. How children learn is a concern today for we can not teach the way we were taught. Teaching through technology must be a practise rather than an occasional occurrence, for sure if there has to be a Wow feature within classrooms.

As teachers we must not use technology as a silicon coating, but with harnessing the power of technology to connect with our students. No more it is about copying and pasting which we have had been doing over the years. For power corrupts politicians so PowerPoint corrupts the teachers if it has just slides and no explanations. For a matter of thought and intelligence, the platform should be to share for show rather than expecting it to be the only parcel for knowledge delivery. There is a certain need to implement a new way of teaching through technology and hence a digital pedagogy is what is required the most. The teachers need to introspect how children may learn in this networked environment. We can't simply take a textbook and deliver it digitally, rather the need here is to explore the power to harness the best via connectivity and creativity to connect.

We just can't actually think and re-discover the chalkboard and make it a smartboard to deliver knowledge. What is required is a novel mindset of

love, care and delivery of priorities for our children within classrooms. We ultimately need a different paradigm for teaching, a different pedagogy which talks about creation, control of chaos, connection to correcting and above all consumption to creation. The teachers need to change their thinking of how they are going to use technology in education.

For sure, we are living in a world of change, there are ample tweets each minute, ample facebook page views each minute. The academic Donald Norman describes skeuomorphism in terms of cultural constraints: interactions with a system that are learned only through culture. The term intensifies the tech world with pride. The world has only been used in the tech industry for a few years, where its meaning has changed, says Dan O'Hara, an academic at Birmingham City University. "Skeumorphs are not strictly something that can be designed," he says. "They occur unintentionally when aesthetic styles are inherited without thinking." The photo views of Flickr which mounts to n' undefined, explore the universal learning of repute. With each minute of over 47,000 app downloads on the apple store encapsulates a new phase of dimensional learning taking place out of the hunger for knowledge. Of course, all these facts did not exist before 2004 by any chance. The availability of data online fascinates the new learner in multiple ways who tend to be a multitasker in pave to grab the unknown. To sound far-fetched but true, the schools over the years have not changed. They have taken the same task to be limited to rows and columns with a teacher at pace. They typically at large have no technology hence there has been no change. There are reports too, "Failed iPad Experiment Shows BYOD Belongs in Schools.", "LA. Cancels iPads-in-the-schools program: a failure of vision, not technology. In spite of all our heavy investments at schools, it appears there is a failure of our strategy or the vision to implement the best of technology in education. And above all, it appears a failure of our pedagogy. One of our mistakes as educators is CTRL + C & CTRL + V. Necessarily as COPY and PASTE for this just can't solve the concerns but expands the issue in particular. This is one of the mistakes we get to govern while implementing technology in our schools.

Similarly, the conclusion goes by fetching the scenario of obvious reasons, which relate to shifting the teaching into a new realm. The core teaching principles having a shift, need an @ctivated model so as to conclude with the no looking back in perfection. The teachers need to be an advocate for holistic education. This transforms the learners in a big way to assist learning and make it happen within the classrooms. Teachers need to keep things simple and do what works for them. For us, the teachers cannot teach the way we were taught. Above all the students, at large, would only like the subject if they like the teacher and this is one of the solitaire truths for any holy classroom in particular. Teachers need to have a wellness routine planning sheet, getting the win-win approach of the happiness index of the students, roll number wise. Indeed, classroom management has been identified as a major concern for teachers and if they don't get along with the learners as bosses or clients with affection, the management of the class appears slang. The teachers in the majority have a wrong notion that classroom management is much to do with discipline only and is limited to the children being quiet in the class, whereas the goals include identification of misconceptions about managing the teaching, the students and the consequences. The teachers of age need to broader the very conception of classroom management and ultimately need to provide a framework among the colleagues for developing their own classroom management plan. Engaging the children in instructions often leads to classroom management but is limited to a classic time only. For having an activated classroom, there has to be a thoughtful physical environment supported by establishing caring relationships and the implementation of engaging instructions.

X
Quality Teaching Ideas

IDEA #1

Change your vocabulary of teaching:
Think different. Children no longer love the
yesteryears' learning of A for Apple, B for Boy and C
for Cat!
They want A for Android, B for Blackberry and C for
Cloud!

IDEA #2

Make use of coloured chalk for writing on the blackboard. Also, explore the possibility of using WHITE Boards and Colored Markers as a practice.

IDEA #3

Be professionally dressed and use a QUALITY PEN. Never hang an ordinary PEN as a Cosmetic Effect!

IDEA #4

Believe in Learning and not TEACHING!

IDEA #5

*Remember you are a TEACHER first, a MATHS, a PHYSICS, or any SUBJECT Teacher!
And keep the passion.*

IDEA #6

*Let the children work in a Partnership- A group of
TWO.
For every answer, let the two decisions about the
answer. The partnership makes 1 and 1 eleven!
For every work and assignment and even queries by
the Teacher!*

IDEA #7

Make ANCHOR charts to SPICE up your classroom.

IDEA #8

*Make use of an EDUCATIONAL TOOL Always when
in Class.*

IDEA #9

*Use the recent example to explain the concept you
are taking as content.*

IDEA #10

Deliver pride in whatever you deliver.

IDEA #11

Gather CONFIDENCE in yourself the first time-
Every time!

IDEA #12

Deliver passion and WOW element while
TEACHING and LECTURING

IDEA #13

Praise your CHILDREN in PUBLIC and always-2
Criticize them in PRIVATE if you ever happen too!

IDEA #14

Deliver the Knowledge With examples/ references
and live coverage of facts.

IDEA #15

Make it a point to share at least ONE
EDUCATIONAL LINK of the day with your kids.

IDEA #16

Please share a story or a report to make them read your eye-balls.

IDEA #17

Always keep some queries on your bucket list to ask from your Students!

IDEA #18

Exchange morning greetings with a personal touch like Hi Ashish, how are you doing!

Using the first name brings rapport building.

IDEA #19

Talk to your students about what happens in your classroom. Give students ownership and responsibility for their success.

IDEA #20

Believe in classroom Innovations regularly. Make Learning a hobby for the kids using TOOLS of interest and everyday usage.

IDEA #21

Create a set of Classroom Courtesy Rules

Let all the students follow the same.

IDEA #22

Avoid disrespectful behaviours. Give a patient hearing to all the children in the class.

IDEA #23

A Classroom has to be a party to excellence in Education. If you show students warmth, respect and interest, they will run through walls for you.

IDEA #24

Think of a Classroom Makeover!

Gone are the days when we think of having ROWS and COLUMNS. Let there be a circular, Face-to-Face,

Semi Circular arrangement of seating where there is no backbencher at all!

IDEA #25

Appeal to the HEART of the Children before their brain. Get emotionally involved with them. Make them emotionally intense.

IDEA #26

Cultivate your engagement meter with the students in the class. Make sure all the children know you well and have at least answered

your queries at least once a week!

IDEA #27

Use the technique of BRAINSTORMING

To explore better learning using the group learning methodology.

IDEA #28

Make use of NLP Techniques within classrooms like **RAPPORT**

Building/ Mirroring/ Matching/ Visualisation and Anchoring.

IDEA #29

Use MIND MAPS

To teach and revise the work done.

IDEA #30

Communicate with students and encourage and focus their writing with a PROMPT!

IDEA #31

Teach Self Awareness about Knowledge. Create a consistent Classroom Routine.

IDEA #32

Create a Culture of Explanation instead of a culture of a correct answer

IDEA #33

Use Questioning Strategies that make all students **THINK** *&* **ANSWER**

IDEA #34

Generate the WOW Experience in the classroom learning/

teaching to catch the eyeballs of the audience. Deliver **PRIDE** *&* **DELIGHT!**

IDEA #35

Use individual Strategies to target students who act out. Recognise and respect each child's attention and interest.

IDEA #36

*Don't teach hard Teach Smart.
Be a Street Smart Teacher!*

Teach them the way they like, not what you want!

IDEA #37

Update yourself with the march of time with knowledge not only in your subject but in general.

Remember you are a TEACHER fir, then an English/ Maths/ Physics or a Hindi Teacher.

IDEA #38

Successful TEACHERS have to have one world life plan!

IMPROVE

Check the last time you taught and the change you incorporated since then!

IDEA #39

Successful Teachers have to have a one-word LIFE Plan:

VISION
To Bring DELIGHT THEIR STUDENTS!

IDEA #40

Try to encapsulate 3Ks'

KODO, KAGNE and KAIZEN *The Japanese philosophy of continuously thinking, acting and improving.*

IDEA #41

Create your cloud presence and make sure you have google counts to impress your audience regularly. Be active on social and professional sites.

IDEA #42

Kick up your classrooms to the next higher orbit using the power of TECHNOLOGY. Make online blogs for students to comment on the day's learning outcome and feedback!

IDEA #43

Commence your lesson on an exciting and enthusiastic note by constantly motivating the students and arousing curiosity among them.

IDEA #44

Share the learning objective with the children. Also, try to know well what students already know. Praise them for their knowledge and honour them for their intelligence!

IDEA #45

Always have some warm-up activity before teaching. This may include moving around the class, like asking each kid in the class to go and shake hands with the very next plus two roll order either way!

IDEA #46

•

Use e-learning to explore or deliver some video on **MOTIVATION** *or* **AWARENESS** *and debate it within the classroom.*

IDEA #47

Appreciate every slight improvement in the class.

Hey, I am excited to be being here in the class. All my students are the best children in the world!

I want all of you guys to get 100% in my subject!

IDEA #48
Put your ego aside.

Be ready to come down to the level of students.

IDEA #49
Be warm and courteous.

Have an approachable nature and treat every student in your class as a

VIP!

IDEA #50

Bridge the digital gap by asking the students and sharing the learning on the use of Technology.

Don't feel shy to ask about ICT/ IT Skills if you need any from the kids.

IDEA #51

Use the presence On CLOUD Via

Dedicated websites like Scribd.com, Webs.com, Instagram Podcast
Blog it Linkedin Twitter add on to your Facebook presence!

IDEA #52 Consider your wellness

Stay hydrated, and don't skip your meals as your

work may demand standing for too long while teaching.

IDEA #53

Never make faces in going for arrangement classes/ Substitute classes; instead, take it as an opportunity

to learn from your students and use that learning as ICE BREAKERS for a routine.

IDEA #54

Try setting high expectations for all the students. They say, "All my

students deserve 100% in my subject".

IDEA #55

Be prepared and organised with every class's content, chapter, and deliberations flow. Never go unprepared.

IDEA #56

*Develop a **STRONG** relationship with the students: A much ahead than taking attendance and time wish interactions.*

IDEA #57

*Carry your water bottle, resource book and markers if needed to explore the best of moments in **TEACHING** without distractions within the classroom.*

IDEA #58

Carry some candies for surprises to the students as a praiseworthy moment/ celebration, if any.

IDEA #59

*Assure to **SING THE BIRTHDAY SONG** for the student in class with the other children. It works wonders!*

IDEA #60

Randomly change the wall hangings/ notices/ charts and tools of teaching in the classrooms to encourage learning with the NEW BUCKET LIST.

IDEA #61

Be a ROCKSTAR Teacher by remembering all the children's names in the class by FIRST NAME and never address them by the ROLL NUMBERS or SIR NAME.

IDEA #62

Have a HOME visit with a prior appointment at least once a SESSION to know more about the child's learning habits.

IDEA #63

Make sure you teach LIFE SKILLS, too, along with the SUBJECT you are assigned to. This would generate a special rapport of yours with your students. May require "Discussing MALALA and OBAMA to dwell interest among them".

IDEA #64

*Wear a **PERFUME** of choice and be a dignified **PERSONALITY** with some personal branding for students' love Street, Smart Teachers!*

IDEA #65

*Always refer to some **REFERENCE BOOKS** and let not be limited to the prescribed ones' including e-books and web references.*

IDEA #66

Do not be limited to

***WORDS OF PRAISE** and **COMMENTS** viz. **CAN DO BETTER** must not be the only **ONLY** feedback/ Remark for the Report Cards..... **PLEASE**.*

IDEA #67

*As a **CLASS TEACHER**, dwell on some innovation while taking attendance. Never bolt a limited proxy or answer codes of **YES SIR** or **PRESENT SIR**. Make some roll out prompts to make it loud and clear.*

IDEA #68

Ask QUESTIONS which 90% of the students MAY answer, not otherwise. The priority must not be to embrace PHOBIA but a CONNECT.

IDEA #69

Conduct QUALITY CIRCLE approach within the classroom with a minimum of 5 members in a group. They must sit together and brainstorm the IDEA and settle with DATA followed by a PRESENTATION by the group.

IDEA #70

Encourage EXPERIENTIAL LEARNING in nearly all subjects of taught to incorporate the learning of Soft Skills, decision making and connect with the nature

IDEA #71

Assure a proper BODY LANGUAGE. It must be well articulated not to send any wrong message to the students. The students observe even the NAIL PAINT of the teachers!

IDEA #72

A TEACHER must respect the DIVERGENT VIEWS of the students in the class. Every child is essential in the class and deserves recognition.

IDEA #73

Be a ROCKSTAR TEACHER by USING TECHNOLOGY in Classrooms to connect with students 24x7.
Make use of your PEN DRIVE more often. Explore the connection using EDUCATIONAL APPS With your clients/ audience!

IDEA #74

Believe in your students that they can do wonders too by little motivation and recognition from your end. Treat them as YOUNG ADULTS, not kids anymore!

IDEA #75

Treat your Students as your real BOSSES around. Remember to satisfy over 40 x 5 sections = 200 bosses every day! Impress them with your deliberations, knowledge and style- once and always!

IDEA #76

Explore COLLABORATIVE learning not TEACHING and make sure you share the learning with a hobby to explore DELIGHT while sharing and learning. Use the phrase "Let us Learn" rather than "Let me TEACH!"

IDEA #77

Limit the usage of the words "TRY", "BUT" and "IF" during your sessions in the classroom as they bring NEGATIVE BELIEF!

IDEA #78

Use references, books by other authors to avoid students' illusion of Sir, it is already in the book, tell us something new!

IDEA #79

Set a MILESTONE CHART for your students' success and your satisfaction as a priority.

Assure all your students score 100% in your subject!

IDEA #80

Calibrate your behavior and teaching skills from time to time by changing your ICE BREAKING strategies and interactive vocabulary.

IDEA #81
Be aware and awake!

You all must have eyes in the back of your Heads! Ask students to collaborate and brainstorm on your classroom's Facebook Page!

IDEA #82

Be attentive and a Repartee to their queries by choice!

IDEA #83

*Believe in the **WIN WIN** situation and **OWNERSHIP** wisdom. My boys and girls are the best!*
*For winners **MAKE** it happen and losers let it **HAPPEN!***

IDEA #84

Never compare and blame the other teachers for their work in public, for the more you blame the more lame you become!

IDEA #85

Admit that you are not perfect. Have a habit to change with the march of time. Forget your yester years as a Student for you can but not teach as you were taught!

IDEA #86

*Admit that you are not **PERFECT***
Make learning to learn your habit rather than an occasional occurrence!

IDEA #87

Explore the
KWINK Analysis (Knowing What I Now Know)

and try manipulating your limitations and Strengths. Work on your limitations to make them as your constructers for betterment.

IDEA #88

Forget the

COMFORT ZONE

Accept challenges and the options for teaching other subjects/ senior classes/ organizing opportunities/ participation and other assignments as a pride!

IDEA #89

Accept 100% responsibility for your class result and the academic climate of your class. This is your key to self-esteem, self- confidence, self-reliance and self respect.

IDEA #90

Practice positive thinking with the students and colleagues

ALL THE TIME

This generates wisdom in your self and rapport among your peers.

IDEA #91

Explore classroom management skills through setting your priorities using the 80/20 rule to your daily tasks and activities. Remember that 80 percent of your results will come from 20 percent of the items on your list. Get your classroom event on your students' calendars by creating a Facebook Event.

IDEA #92

Minimize your distractions within the classrooms. Avoid checking messages/ calls/ posts/ updates while in your classroom. A ready reckoner student friendly teacher does not even carry a mobile phone in the classroom ever.

IDEA #93

Act like a ZEN MASTER not a RING MASTER

Let the students in the class follow your spiritual learning and Blessings instead of being a HARD TASK MASTER.

IDEA #94

Be SMART! Systematic: In teaching Meticulous: In Working Artistic: In Presentation Realistic: In Calibration

Tactful: In Classroom Management

IDEA #95

Calibrate your behavior as per the scenario of the classroom situation. Never carry a grudge or a disliking for any student ever. Forgive and Forget with some golden words like May GOD Bless you!

IDEA #96

Stop being responsive. Instead, protect your time and energy for the things that matter most. If you are finding an interesting discussion time, ask students to simply continue the discussion on

Facebook and move on.

IDEA #97

Incorporate a procedure of a T-MAIL (Teachers' Mail Box)

A note to the teacher on some query or an experience to share in private.

IDEA #98

*Use the **POST-IT NOTES** on*

classroom walls against a name. It can be a praise or a personal improvement note for the child. Both by the teacher to the child and vice-versa!

IDEA #99

Have a conversation Notebook with the students in circulation within the class. This may be a personal small note book to the teacher by the kids with a special note on queries and achievements.

IDEA #100 Share **MORNING GREETINGS**

On a personal note during get together moments and during the Assembly hours to develop rapport with the students.

IDEA #101

Share a meal with the students during lunch hours and breaks. The kids enjoy sharing the food and love being praised on taste and share the enjoyment for trust and rapport building.

IDEA #102

Always act like the TEACHER you always knew you could be. Take a back seat in your classroom and virtually be a learner in your class. Use APPS like WORD OF THE DAY, THIS DAY IN HISTORY to create small but fun nuggets of learning on a regular basis.

IDEA #103

One should be inspiring the children all the time and every time in the class. Be like a ROCKSTAR to the students in class with some WOW factors exhibited!

IDEA #104

Be flexible about the choices and the assignments you make in the classroom with liberty to the students to make decisions and curate knowledge on their own.

IDEA #105

Install a procedure of 5S Quality Plan and action

Seiri; Sort, Clearing, Classify

Seiton; Straighten, Simplify, Set

in order, Configure

Seiso; Sweep, shine, Scrub,

Clean and Check

Seiketsu; Standardize,

stabilize, Conformity

Shitsuke; Sustain, self

discipline, custom and practice

IDEA #106

Exercise CANDO in the classroom on a periodic basis

-

Cleanup Arrange Neatness Discipline Ongoing Improvement

IDEA #107

Never fear taking calculated risks which may include going for substitution/ arrangement/ replacement classes or managing a different subject assignment.

IDEA #108

Never dwell on the past Over failure and unjustified lesson deliberations. Believe in the best of your children and match their confidence with making learning happen through interactions and deliberations.

IDEA #109

*Don't make the same mistake twice. The students may not entertain you as a good teacher. Instead ask them for help and assistance particularly mapping on use of **TECHNOLOGY** in the classroom or other tools for learning.*

IDEA #110

Do not expect immediate results from your children. Keep the level of confidence high and motivate the children of great expectations and a win win approach.

IDEA #111

Accept and implement change on a periodic manner and don't shy away. Implement the best of technology with the support of the students in class.

Remember, teachers are no longer the sages on the stage but the guides on the floor!

IDEA #112

Master over your fears of classroom management and distractions within classrooms. Build a rapport with the children over time with your PERSONALITY and GOOD Vocabulary.

IDEA #113

Always be willing to evolve as a Good Teacher with expertise to make learning happen and a difference every time you enter the classroom.

IDEA #114

Cultivate a common interest in the class. Let all students prepare to learn with common objectives.

IDEA #115
A sense of humour helps.

IDEA #116

Never compare one child with the other in the class. No one wins the comparison game. Treat every child in the class as a Unique child with a different learning preference and a style.

IDEA #117

Be a Rainmaker not only for your Class but also for your school where you teach!

The term 'Rainmaker' was first used by Native Americans to connote a medicine man who by various rituals and incantations sought to literally make it rain.

IDEA #118

Be a HUMAN BEING first and foremost. Treat every child as a human being too! Be human and understand the reality. Limit your home work assignments to being human.

IDEA #119

Intend to listen to your audience and to the answers to the questions you have asked not only with your ears but also with your eyes. Listen with your whole body. Show engagement and signal through your eyes. Good teachers are invariably good listeners.

IDEA #120

Make sure you ask Pertinent Questions in the class and also give the same in the question papers/ writing/ oral examinations. They must match the learning imparted and must not be out of discussion.

IDEA #121

Be Prepared for any conversations, meetings, presentations and explanations. This is to project a good image of your Teaching Skills and personality.

IDEA #123

*Concentrate on your TOUCH TIME
And execute
Proper TIME MANAGEMENT during deliberations and classroom project assignments.*

IDEA #124

As a Teacher it is important to measure the LEARNING OUTCOME after every class. Analyze the feedback and the improvements required after every session and the module.

IDEA #125

As a TEACHER always be a Maven- An Accumulator of Knowledge, A Connector – To deliver Knowledge and and Evangelist- To develop followers and promote the idea to excel via the shared knowledge.

IDEA #126

Quit Whining!
Over Arrangements/ Substitutions/ Replacement Classes/ Attendance Register updating/ Extra hours of waiting/ teaching/ Meeting and the teaching of young boys and girls of various attributes.

IDEA #127

Learn to say NO.
Do say NO when you think it is practically IMPOSSIBLE for the task or the assignment to be done. Never commit false promises with the children which you think is cosmetic and unreal for execution.

IDEA #128

Prepare a
TO-DO List
For your classroom lessons as per your planned work or assignment for the week. Make preparations. Carry proper educational tools in the classroom and delegate responsibilities for a nice and friendly learning climate within the classroom.

IDEA #129

As a Teacher always try to do more by doing less. Be a multitasked person using the power of technology

and support from the students. You may be teaching, observing, commenting on a topic and at the same time checking the learning outcome and the behavioral skills of the children in the class using a formative assessment in order.

IDEA #130

Encapsulate COURTESY and HUMILITY. Courtesy for all the students in the class and Humility with the parents and colleagues. Never take pride of your knowledge and be helpful to all as a ready reckoner!

IDEA #131

Be Proactive. Learn to prepare your lessons and assignments with the taste of the children and manage their mood swings

with a delight of knowledge sharing to match their interest and likings.

IDEA #132

Never loose touch with your learning and be prepared and planned with the flow of execution and idea

sharing for the class to deliver. Never go unprepared and wear a smile always.

IDEA #133

Communicate beyond the parent-teacher meeting using the power of technology. Use e-diaries, make the best use of ERP and other communication medium to inform the win- win attributes of the students in class.

IDEA #134

Have a beautiful planner in the class. Students love colourful images and ideas quoted as TO DO Things in the class. Innovation is

what they love in making and activation.

IDEA #135

Have an orderly and color coded classroom with much of spectrum of learning

tools, charts and images. The classroom should be a hub for learning and excitement.

IDEA #136

Have position management: A place for everything and everything in its place.

IDEA #137

Every teacher must and must have a TOOL BOX in the classroom. A ready reckoner with stuff which may include, extra chalk, duster, charts, tools for learning and reference books.

IDEA #138

Teachers must give a reminder to focus on what

is most important on a continuous basis.

IDEA #139

Unleash the master within and deliver your best of mind and skills in explaining the concept. Never take things lightly, if required for some reason, don't teach. Ask the kids to discuss among themselves over some incident or yesterday's football match.

IDEA #140

Master the art of story telling. The students love and appreciate learning via stories and incidences. This leaves an everlasting mark and impression on their minds with a lesson!

IDEA #141

Have a Conversation and practice relentlessly and internalize your content so that you may deliver the deliberation as comfortably as having an interaction with a close buddy!

IDEA #142

Conduct Class Assemblies on a frequent basis so as to build and deliver spiritual quotient with the children. This helps them becoming emotionally strong.

IDEA #143

Organise a small CLASS Library with some reference books for circulation within the class. It always works wonders when they take the liberty to access them on choice when required during the learning process.

IDEA #144

Bring into the class any outside object in order to intrigue them and make them learn in the form of a QUIZ over the object.

IDEA #145

Reach your classroom with in a different attire away from usual days to impart knowledge and grip the attention of the students as a choice!

IDEA #146

Adjust your volume and pitch according to the issues and deliberations being addressed in the class.

IDEA #147

Point out the most dis- interested child of your class and ask him for his opinion on the topic being addressed in the class.

IDEA #148

Start your class with an innovative and capturing statement or words Like
A Quote from HARRY Potter!

IDEA #149

Must explore and learn to exercise free will with responsible actions in the class for the students to emulate.

IDEA #150

Converse with the students in the class and around the campus in an unhurried way. Pause frequently and make sure the listening is happening from the other hand with no fear and dis- interest. Pace with the learning of the students.

IDEA #151

Encourage your students to share what they learn on a regular basis.

IDEA #152

With every lesson make students need to participate in their learning via assignments, survey sheets and oral quizzes.

IDEA #153

Encourage critical thinking and participation using workshops/ webinars/ skype sessions to bring learning happen with joy and commitment.

IDEA #154

Let students MODEL you as a teacher.

Practice JOY, FUN and Perfection.

IDEA #155

Always start with

INTIMATION
to students about the topic, what they are going to learn, teach them, let them use it and then ask what they have learned. Also discuss homework before wrapping up the class as a priority.

IDEA #156

Modify the dynamics of the class by pairing the students together. As a teacher, make sure you control who is being paired with whom.

IDEA #157

Always give limits for each task. Just do not let them free to TRY at leisure. An assignment in a given time and a timely submission must be a priority and must be a common desire for all.

IDEA #158

Watch for signs of Boredom on a regular basis and change your teaching interface accordingly. Stop the lesson if you observe the students "Sleeping with their Eyes open!"

IDEA #159

Condense your comments on Students to avoid indirect criticism and dwelling unwillingness to learn otherwise.

IDEA #160

*Realize no one likes **GLOOMY** people and your observation in the class as a **LAZY** teacher would go negative for their interest in the learning.*

IDEA #161

Keep your students busy with group assignments instead of an individual assignment. Ask them to build real projects so that they may be used on a later stage in life or for other classes.

IDEA #162

Have a video recording of the classroom session with a specific or a difficult topic. This may be a good way to review lessons from an outside perspective further. It may also serve as a ready reckoner online, once uploaded!

IDEA #163

Stop Arguing and causing trouble. Let it go approach may be the best for you as a TEACHER. Forgive and Forget.

IDEA #164

Share the learning from attending a SKILL DEVELOPMENT workshop or share the learning you have had with the colleagues in the recent "Enrichment Meeting"

• 92 •

IDEA #165

Take a break!
Get the best out of yourself with sports or singing a song to make a lively environment filled with comic and entertainment within the classroom.

IDEA #166

Take a Qualification using some of the online resources and make it public the students. Give them the option to follow your learning.

IDEA #167

Use links like SCRIBD.COM for sharing ideas/ concepts/ write-ups and get a follow stream at a 24x4 approach. Avoid social networking connectivity.

IDEA #168

Carry your smile always. If you see someone without a smile, give them one of yours!

IDEA #169

Love your students and make them feel they are the most important people for you. This brings their liking for you and their being in the classrooms.

IDEA #170

Assume your students to be the best children in the world. With no comparison so at all. Compare them with themselves of yesterday and the next day they should and would be!

IDEA #171

Assume that your students are the best of the students in the world. Meet to their expectations by delivering the best and make them feel so by giving them hour, recognition and pride. Praise what and when you can!

IDEA #172

Display the classroom rules and enforce them consistently. Never let it go without practice.

IDEA #173

Use positive language with no negative words and negative belief. Be win-win all the time, every time.

IDEA #174

Make your students responsible for their own learning environment. Let them question the learning with no fear of failure but an encourage participation by all.

IDEA #175

Make it a point to avoid confrontations in front of the students in class. Let it roll with peace and prosperity of understanding.

IDEA #176

Connect with the Parents through the students and they must be informed about the connect. The fear is natural and let that be there.

IDEA #177

Assure and assume the Attention of every student in the class before the lesson begins. This may be done using ICE BREAKERS or using pointers of easy questions which 90% of the students may answer!

IDEA #178

Always use simple verbal reprimands but in PRIVATE when the misbehavior occurs. This leads to understanding the child and his modeling of the behavior is achieved.

IDEA #179 Avoid the threats like

"I shall call your parents" or

"I shall take you to the PRINCIPAL"

This dilutes your importance and recognition.

IDEA #180

De intervene as soon as possible for any even if, a trivial matter of misbehavior among the children in class. Ignoring means enhancing the trouble.

IDEA #181

Let the students learn to strive for greater self-control during situational analysis within classrooms.

IDEA #182

Activate a ROLE PLAY based learning and knowledge. Make the maximum participation possible by the students.

IDEA #183

Never get emotional with any student in class. Your profession is of a TEACHER and not simply a PARENT. You need to occupy spectrum of discipline with AWE- Respect with Fear- on Demand!

IDEA #184

Spend so much time improving yourself that you have no time for staff Room politics and to criticize others. Believe in your wisdom towards excellence!

IDEA #185

Be so strong with your words and commitment that nothing can disturb your peace of mind in the classroom and in the school. Stay away from classroom distractions instead try implementing solutions to every concern in the class.

IDEA #186

Talk health, happiness and hygiene towards prosperity to every student you meet. Make them feel good every time they meet you. Inspire them with good words, motivation and inspiration.

IDEA #187

Have a dedicated time for PEP TALK, ASSEMBLY TALK and above all some ZEN Talk with the students on life, living and wisdom! Discussion realities attached to LIFE as a Mystery!

IDEA #188

*Be as enthusiastic about the success of each and every student of yours as you are for yourself. Make the recognition public via all means of sharing including **SOCIAL MEDIA**
It counts!*

IDEA #189

*Activate **CLASS WISE** Assembly and invite the parents to witness the same with participation of each and every student of the class.*

IDEA #190

*Invite **PARENTS** for **FAMILY HOUR** once a month for 10 minutes **ONE TO ONE** with you and the other subject Teachers together with the Child and give him praises of count and wisdom.*

IDEA #191

*Send **PRAISES** to parents whose students perform good out of average. Send them Congratulations Card and tag them as a **WINNER** Parent of the week! On the school's FB Page.*

IDEA #192

Once a week ask your children to write a love letter to themselves. Praising them for their great doings and acknowledging their wrong doings. Make them read and share the findings with their friends.

IDEA #193

Make the classroom routine routed with the phrases:

I can I will I care

All I want is within me, I am confident, I can do it, YES!

IDEA #194

Ability comes from doing and not WATCHING. As a teacher let this happen in classrooms through role plays, experiential learning and participative learning.

IDEA #195

Encourage COMPETENCY
Not COMPETITION
Let the competency of individuals be explored via

formative assessments routed and guided by the teachers.

IDEA #196

*Happy Teachers Change the world of learning in the classrooms. Be happy and excited with every moment of joy and replicate that in your children while teaching. Develop your **HAPPINESS QUOTIENT.***

IDEA #197

WHO and HOW you are educates the child more than what you teach. Make your presence felt and explored in class by your attributes.

IDEA #198

Don't Walk the talk, Don't Talk the talk, Instead

WORK The talk!

IDEA #199

Treat every classroom As

A LEARNING WALK!

• 101 •

Never take arrangement or a substitution classes as a liability instead make it a learning Opportunity from the kids!

ABOUT THE AUTHOR

Dheeraj Mehrotra, MS, MPhil, PhD (Education Management) honoris causa., a white and a yellow belt in SIX SIGMA, a Certified NLP Business Diploma holder, is an Educational Innovator, Author, with expertise in Six Sigma In Education, Academic Audits, Neuro-Linguistic Programming (NLP), Total Quality Management In Education, an Experiential Educator, a CBSE Resource towards School Assessment (SQAA), CCE, JIT, Five S, and KAIZEN. He has authored over 40 books on Computer Science for ICSE/ ISC/ CBSE Students, over 60 books of academic interest for education excellence, and Six Sigma. A former Principal at De Indian Public School, New Delhi, (INDIA) with an ample teaching experience of over Two Decades, he is a certified Trainer for Quality Circles/ TQM in Education and QCI Standards for School Accreditation. He has developed over 150 FREE EDUCATIONAL MOBILE Apps for the Google Play Store exclusively for Teachers, Students, and Parents. This work has been recognised by the LIMCA BOOK OF RECORDS & INDIA BOOK OF RECORDS as the only Indian to draw that feast. Dr Mehrotra is presently working as a PRINCIPAL at KUNWARS GLOBAL SCHOOL, Lucknow, in India. He has conducted over 1000 workshops globally on "Excellence In Education" integrated with Total Quality Management and Six Sigma, Technology Integration in Education (TIE), Developing towards being ROCKSTAR TEACHERS, including Cyberspace, Cyber Security, Classroom Management, School Leadership & Management, and Innovative teaching within classrooms via Mind Maps, NLP and Experiential Learning in Academics. He is an active TEDx speaker and can be viewed on the youtube TEDx channel. As a premium UDEMY Instructor, he has also developed over 450 courses and is catering to over 8 Lakh students from 180 plus countries.

He can be visited at www.authordheerajmehrotra.com

BOOKS BY THE SAME AUTHOR

www.authordheerajmehrotra.com

•

THE 200 HABITS OF
HIGHLY
EFFECTIVE
LEARNERS
Making Learning a Habit
DR. DHEERAJ MEHROTRA

101
SCHOOL
MANAGEMENT
STRATEGIES
Towards EFFECTIVE
QUALITY MANAGEMENT
System in Schools
DR. DHEERAJ
MEHROTRA

DR. DHEERAJ MEHROTRA
99 EFFECTIVE WAYS
TO MANAGE YOUR SCHOOLS
POST COVID-19

PRIORITY LEARNING FOR EDUCATORS
It is worth knowing now!
digital body Language
WORK ETHICS FOR TEACHERS
TEACHER'S TOOLKIT POST COVID
TOWARDS EXCELLENCE IN TEACHING & LEARNING
200 WOW TEACHING IDEAS
NLP FOR TEACHERS
Towards Quality Teaching Skills
Teachers' Favourite Teaching Strategies That Work
APPLYING SIX SIGMA WITHIN CLASSROOMS
Buy now at amazon.in
DR. DHEERAJ MEHROTRA
EXPERIENTIAL LEARNING FOR EDUCATORS
TOWARDS QUALITY LITERACY FOR ALL
Academic Audits In Schools
What, Why & How?

TOWARDS EXCELLENCE IN
TEACHING & LEARNING
200
WOW TEACHING
IDEAS
DR. DHEERAJ MEHROTRA
200 WOW
Teaching
Ideas
Available at
amazon